20th century icons
FASHION

ISBN 1 899791 92 2

First published in 1999 by Absolute Press,
Scarborough House 29 James Street West,
Bath, Somerset, BA1 2BT, England
T 01225 316013 **F** 01225 445836
E info@absolutepress.demon.co.uk

Icons selected by John Rocha
Text by Verity McIlveen
Series Editor: Camilla Ford
Design: Christine Leech

Printed by Phase Print Ltd, Underwood, England

20th century icons
FASHION
selected by John Rocha

Acknowledgments

Thanks are due to all of the individuals, companies and organisations who helped towards the production of this book. Many provided material and information that was greatly appreciated. In particular, Absolute Press and Terrence Higgins Trust would like to thank the following for their generous commitment to the project.

London Features International Ltd
3 Boscobel Street
London NW8 8PS
T +44 (0) 20 7723 4204
F +44 (0) 20 7723 9201
E admin@lfi.co.uk
W www.lfi.co.uk

The Kobal Collection
4th Floor
184 Drummond Street
London NW1 3HP
T +44 (0) 171 383 0011
F +44 (0) 171 383 0044

British Film Institute
21 Stephen Street
London W1P 2LN
T +44 (0) 171 255 1444
F +44 (0) 171 580 7503
E caroline.ellis@bfi.org.uk

Hulton Getty Picture Collection
Unique House
21-31 Woodfield Road
London W9 2BA
T +44 (0) 171 266 2662
F +44 (0) 171 266 3154
E info@getty-images.com
W www.hultongetty.com

Big Pictures
9 St John Street
London EC1M 4AA
T +44 (0) 171 250 3555
F +44 (0) 171 250 0033

Monitor Syndication
(incorporates the City Syndication library)
17 Old Street
London EC1V 9HL
T +44 (0) 171 253 7071
F +44 (0) 171 250 0966

Contents

Terrence Higgins Trust

I'd like to extend my personal thanks on behalf of the Terrence Higgins Trust to everybody involved in the *20th Century Icons* series of books, particularly John Rocha who has devoted not only his talent, time and effort into producing this wonderful book but has also agreed to donate his royalties to the Terrence Higgins Trust. This generosity has been matched by Absolute Press who will be making a donation to equal the royalties.

I have been involved personally in the fight against HIV and AIDS since the disease first appeared in the UK in 1982 and the Terrence Higgins Trust was founded. Our work to stop the spread of HIV and support people living with and affected by HIV and AIDS is as important now as it was then.

Last year a record number of people were diagnosed as having HIV and the Terrence Higgins Trust provided services to over 11,000 people – many of them living not only with this terrible disease, but also facing discrimination and poverty. It is thanks to the generosity of John Rocha, everybody else involved in the preparation of this book and the concern of people like you that the Terrence Higgins Trust is able to undertake its vital work.

Nick Partridge OBE
Chief Executive

'Truly stylish women are the opposite of a fashion victim: they are leaders, not followers.'

John Rocha

John Rocha

Born in Hong Kong, of Chinese and Portuguese descent,
John Rocha moved to London to study fashion. His graduation
collection featured Irish linen, which inspired him to visit Ireland
and eventually move to Dublin, where he has lived for the past
19 years and where he works closely with his wife and
business partner, Odette.

In 1994, John was awarded the prestigious title of British Designer
of the Year. The John Rocha design operation has expanded over
the years and now incorporates many varied projects.

Spring-Summer 1997 saw the successful introduction of the John
Rocha Jeans range for men and women, a collection aimed at the
casual market with its own branded identity and style.

In 1997, in partnership with the world famous Waterford
Crystal, John launched an extensive range of contemporary
table-top crystal specifically aimed at the modern crystal market.
'John Rocha at Waterford Crystal' has proved a great success
throughout America, the UK and Australia. 1998 saw the addition
of an exclusive range of modern crystal lighting, and in 1999,
new stemware and home accessories were introduced.

John opened his first store in London in 1998. Situated in Sloane Avenue, SW3 the store reflects the unique fusion of Chinese and Celtic style that has become synonymous with John. It is a showcase for both his mainline collections, plus John Rocha Jeans, John Rocha at Waterford Crystal and John Rocha Home Accessories.

1999 saw two major new projects reach fruition. The first was the opening of The Morrison, a new hotel in the heart of Dublin. John has been working on the concept and design for the hotel over the past year and has achieved stunning results. In April, following two years of design and development, the new Virgin Atlantic Airways uniform was launched, designed by John Rocha and worn by 5,000 staff and crew worldwide.

Foreword

My idea of a fashion icon is of unmistakable individuality,
of someone who is instantly recognisable. Truly stylish women
are the opposite of fashion victims: they are leaders, not followers.
All my favourite fashion icons are style pioneers who achieve
individual elegance by using and changing fashion, moulding it
to suit their own type of beauty, their own personality and taste.
Their glamour is a personal radiance that comes from inner
strength, confidence and self-knowledge. Because they
transcend passing trends, they all remain, whatever their age,
whatever era they lived in, eternally young and modern:
an inspiration for today.

John Rocha

Coco Chanel

1883-1971

Pioneer of the LBD (Little Black Dress), and the woman who gave us suntans, ladies' trousers and No. 5 perfume, Coco Chanel did much to establish Chanel's timeless appeal .

Aiming to create practical clothing, which would deliver freedom, simplicity and comfort, she transformed wool jersey – previously only used as underwear fabric – and used it to make dresses. Her signature suits, with boxy jackets, contrasting bias edging and brass buttons were inspired by the crew's uniforms on the Duke of Westminster's yacht, (where she spent time as his mistress) though her fixation with comfortable arm movement often had her ripping the sleeves off them in an effort to obtain a perfect fit. Traditional accessories then, as now, included pearls, gold chains, quilted handbags and two-tone shoes. 'Luxury', she insisted 'is not the opposite of poverty, it's the opposite of vulgarity.'

Julie Christie

b.1941

Julie Christie was born in Assam, India, on the tea plantation owned by her father.

Julie Christie captured the essence of the glamorous, free spirited '60s in her role as a Mod and radiant sexual butterfly in the film *Darling* (1965), for which she won a British Film Academy Award and an Oscar.

Credited with having as many American fans as The Beatles, Christie first achieved fame in the popular '60s British TV serial, *A for Andromeda*. When she became romantically involved with Warren Beatty in 1971, they co-starred in numerous commercial successes including *Shampoo* (1975), *Heaven Can Wait* (1978) and Robert Altman's *McCabe and Mrs Miller* (1971), before Christie went on to opt for more alternative, art-house cinema roles. She can be seen in Kenneth Branagh's recent production of *Hamlet*.

Much of her appeal, however, lies in the fact that she is something of a role model for today's single, independent woman. On the demise of her relationship with Beatty, she was heard to remark 'Men don't want any responsibility, and neither do I.'

Isabelle Adjani

b.1955

Bubbling with underlying passion, and displaying the cool glamour and icy allure associated with the typical French actress, Algerian-German born Isabelle Adjani has made a lasting impression on the French silver screen, with roles in *Camille Claudel* (1989) and *La Reine Margot* (1995) which both won her the César (the French Oscar equivalent).

Hollywood, however, has yet to recognise her potential. Putting her love life first, she turned down roles in *Basic Instinct* and *Indecent Proposal* during her much publicised affair with Daniel Day-Lewis, reportedly saying 'Cinema was no longer the most important thing for me. I am one of those actors who, when they are in love, forget everything else.'

Adjani's style appeal is perhaps best illustrated by the fact that when she wears one of her favourite fragrances, Christian Dior's Diorissimo (the other being Rahat Loukoum by Serge Lutens), she is a bit of a show-stopper. 'When I wear it in England,' she says, 'people stop me in the street.'

Greta Garbo

1905–1990

Garbo's initial sound scene in *Anna Christie* (1930) was the longest, continuous sound take of the time.

As one of the better-looking employees in the department store she worked in as a teenager, Garbo was chosen to appear in a publicity film chosen by the store. It was called *How Not To Dress*.

The personification of all that was alluring and yet unattainable in movie stars, Greta Garbo has remained an enduring icon of beauty and modern femininity.

Bursting onto the Hollywood scene from her native Sweden at the age of 19, Garbo influenced the appearance of a whole generation of women when she signed up with movie giant MGM. Her tremulous voice, expressive eyes and beautiful face appealed to audiences all over the world and earned her the title of 'The Swedish Sphinx', while her dramatic screen presence made her America's highest paid woman of the mid-'30s and won her an Honorary Academy Award in 1954 for her 'unforgettable screen performances.'

Garbo's famous mystique was further heightened by her withdrawal from society on her retirement in 1942. More legend than actress, Cecil Beaton wrote of her appeal as an 'elusive and haunting sensitivity'.

Susan Sarandon

b.1946

Susan Sarandon is an actress of long standing, but it is her more recent portrayals of intelligent and sensually vivacious older women that have earned her the most admirers.

Sarandon's flaming red hair and wide-eyed looks first hit the big time when she starred alongside Cher, Jack Nicholson, and Michelle Pfeiffer in *The Witches of Eastwick* (1987). It was her mature style and sassy appeal that the public loved, and this was substantiated further in *Bull Durham* (1988), hitting an all-time high in the 1991 smash *Thelma and Louise*, although it was *Dead Man Walking* (1995), a film based on the autobiographical story of Sister Helen Prejean, that won her the much coveted Oscar.

Jackie Onassis

1929-1994

With her trademark 'flipped up' hair by Kenneth and signature big sunglasses, white gloves and simple white coat, Jackie Onassis was the personification of elegance, and her style is still revered today.

Her reign as America's first lady saw Onassis become a fashion icon, famous for her boxy shift dresses and the pillbox-style hats created for her by her milliner, Halston. During the Kennedy years, Diana Vreeland of *Harpers Bazaar* and designer Oleg Cassini became her number one style mentors. Her informal, youthful spirit brought beauty, intelligence, and cultivated taste to a White House that had not seen a young wife and children of a President in half a century, and her formal but fashionable flair caught the imagination of the American public. After her husband's assassination in Dallas in1963, Jackie's dignity and courage won her the admiration of the world. At her funeral in 1994 her son John, described three of her attributes: 'love of words, the bonds of home and family, and her spirit of adventure.'

Madonna

b.1958

One of
Madonna's
early efforts
at film making
involved
the frying of
an egg on
her stomach.

On arriving in
New York,
Mads jumped
in a cab,
saying "Take
me where the
action is." She
was left in
Times Square
with $35.

Madonna Ciccone's chameleon-like nature has withstood the scrutiny of a generation always hungry for change, to earn her enduring iconic status.

In her '80s heyday, Madonna's combination of vulgarity and shrewdness, made her an arguably ambiguous symbol of new feminism. At the turn of the decade, Jean Paul Gaultier's pink satin corset with conical breasts became the most famous incarnation of Madonna's dynamic transformations. Others included her lace and torn denim look in the 'Like A Virgin' video, the hard, punky image she adopted for the cover of her debut album, 'Madonna' (1983), and her glamorous Marilyn Monroe portrayal in the 'Material Girl' era.

After the launch of her controversial book *Sex*, the singer did a complete volte face to portray Eva Péron in the 1997 film *Evita*, wearing sophisticated '40s inspired couture. Her favourite designers include Dolce & Gabbana, Jean Paul Gaultier and Gianni Versace and she is a regular at Voyage, the members' only shop in the Fulham Road.

Grace Kelly

1928-1982

The cool elegance of Grace Kelly can be seen at its smouldering best in the Hitchcock films of the '50s. The ultimate glamourpuss, her film career was brief but dazzling, including roles in classics like *High Noon* (1952) and *The Country Girl* (1951) for which her performance opposite Bing Crosby earned her an Oscar, confirming her place in the Hollywood firmament.

Kelly left the glitz of Tinseltown to embark upon a fairy-tale marriage to Prince Rainier III of Monaco, becoming Her Serene Highness, Princess Grace of Monaco. Although she had three children, reports from biographers and friends indicate that the Princess was unhappy in her new life. In 1982, the car she was travelling in with her daughter, Stephanie, then 17, crashed down a steep embankment. Stephanie survived, but tragically, Grace died the next day.

Caroline Bessette-Kennedy

1966-1999

Hailed as a style leader by the international press, Caroline Bessette-Kennedy, wife of John F. Kennedy Jr, was often compared with her late mother-in-law, Jacqueline Kennedy Onassis. It was not only her beauty and sophistication that warranted the comparison, but her work for charity and the ferocity with which she protected her and her husband's privacy.

Her long blonde hair and six-foot stature afforded Bessette much attention even prior to her meeting with Kennedy, and among her former beaux were a Calvin Klein model, a pro-hockey player and the heir to the Benetton fortune. Shortly before her 1996 marriage to Kennedy, who she met when both were jogging through Central Park, she resigned from her job at Calvin Klein. Three years later the press-shy publicist died tragically in a plane crash, along with her sister, Lauren, and her husband, who piloted the aircraft.

Helena Christensen

b.1968

An original Supermodel, Helena Christensen started modelling at the age of nine. Her adaptable beauty, derived from her Peruvian mother and Danish father, has seen her regularly featured in advertising campaigns for Armani, Karl Lagerfeld and Versace. Prestigious contracts with Cover Girl cosmetics, Victoria's Secret lingerie and English chain store Dorothy Perkins have kept her profile on the rise. Designer John Galliano said of her appeal, 'She fills clothes with life and fire.'

Christensen rocketed to fame and fortune when she left home to pursue a modelling career in Paris, shortly after winning the title of Miss Denmark in 1986. A shoot for French *Elle* with photographer Friedemann Hauss was swiftly followed by a cover for British *Vogue*, and soon Helena was a household name, along with the other forerunners of Supermodel culture, Naomi, Kate, Cindy, Christy and Elle, although she generally steers clear of off-camera publicity, stating 'Real life starts when I stop being a model.'

Diana Rigg

b.1938

Voted the sexiest TV star of all time, Diana Rigg was best known for her Emmy award-winning role as *The Avengers'* leather clad seductress, Emma Peel. A forerunner of feminism, she was in person just as blunt and outspoken as her TV character when it came to marriage issues and women's lib.

Though Rigg starred in the Bond film, *On Her Majesty's Secret Service* shortly after leaving *The Avengers*, it was her career as a whole that mattered most to her, and she fought against becoming typecast, turning down many roles that had her carrying guns. She undertook some of her best stage work in the '70s and was one of the first major actors to appear nude on stage in the play *Abelard and Heloise*. The resulting controversy had her named one of the year's best actresses by the London Critics' Circle, and when the play was brought to the United States she received a Tony nomination for Best Actress in a Dramatic Play.

In the '90s, Rigg has returned to the stage to play some of the most demanding roles of her career.

Liv Tyler

b.1977

The sense of glamorous drama surrounding Liv Tyler is heightened by the story of how she discovered, at the age of eight, that rock star Steven Tyler of Aerosmith was her real father. On their first meeting, she mistook him for Mick Jagger's son.

Actress Liv Tyler is one of the most youthfully entrancing stars in Hollywood today. Her dark, tumbling tresses, rich eyes and full lips made her the star of Aerosmith's music video for 'Crazy', though it was as a model that she originally burst onto the New York scene in her teens.

Feature films followed, and Tyler's most tantalising role, and the one that rocketed her to international fame, was as Lucy in Bernardo Bertolucci's *Stealing Beauty* (1996). The legendary director, on launching the film in Cannes said 'I would like to introduce you to the star of my next movie, and my muse.' Her fate as a star was sealed.

At the age of 22, Tyler has four more films to her credit, including *Armageddon* (1998) and *Cookie's Fortune* (1999). In an interview with Helena Christensen in *Nylon* magazine she was asked about the combination of vulnerability and strength in her chosen roles. She said 'All I ever do is trust my heart and my instincts. Sometimes you read a script and something in it just connects to you personally.'

Audrey Hepburn

1929-1993

At the mention of her name, saucer-eyed gamine chic, flat ballet pumps, turtlenecks and slim capri pants will undoubtedly spring to mind. Heralded as a feminine ideal, Audrey Hepburn has had numerous accolades, from *Harpers & Queen* vote as 'the most fascinating woman of our time' to inclusion in *People* magazine's 1990 poll of the 50 most beautiful people in the world.

Trained as a ballet dancer, the *Breakfast at Tiffany's* (1961) star's first success came when she was chosen to star on stage in *Gigi* (1951). Hollywood recognised her ethereal, swan-like beauty, which went further than skin-deep, and a sparkling screen career followed.

Designer and friend, Hubert de Givenchy couldn't have put it better when he said 'There is no woman alive who does not dream of looking like Audrey Hepburn.' Her waif-like style still provides inspiration for admirers the world over and, like Coco Chanel, she changed not only the way women dressed, but also their self-perception. Her style has proved timeless and her influence on contemporary fashion incomparable.

Bianca Jagger

b.1945

Considered the world's best-dressed human-rights representative, Bianca Jagger's first claim to fame was her 1971 marriage to Rolling Stone, Mick Jagger when, as a regular on the glitterati scene at the infamous '70s nightclub Studio 54, she enjoyed the archetypal jet set lifestyle.

The daughter of a wealthy import-export merchant, her early career as an actress has long been overshadowed by her famous marriage and her political activism. Her first protest, sparked soon after her divorce from Mick in 1979, was when she witnessed a raid on a refugee camp in Honduras by Salvadoran soldiers. In her championing of the causes of 'forgotten people', Jagger is now more likely to make headlines for her statements on crime victims than for her hemlines. Her current cause found her at the wrong end of a gun, when in 1998 Serbian forces interrogated her during a TV film expedition to Kosovo.

Brigitte Bardot

b.1934

The 'sex kitten' moniker was created for Brigitte Bardot. Known as BB (which the French pronounce bébé), her potent mix of sensuality and natural childlike charm made her an icon of sexual liberation in the '50s and '60s.

With her Beat-style narrow trousers and tight black sweaters, combined with deshabillé hair and girly gingham dresses, Bardot inspired countless imitators both on screen and off. In her first internationally acclaimed film, *And God Created Woman* (1956) directed by husband Roger Vadim, Bardot popularised flat ballet pumps and set a trend for going sock-free. In the film *Viva Maria* (1965) Bardot's Edwardian dress was mirrored in fashion across the world.

Although Bardot has legendary status as one of the cinema's greatest stars, the actress, whose first ambition was to become a dancer, wrote of her debut cinema appearance in her 1996 autobiography 'If there is hell on earth, this was it!' Her stormy private life led to a suicide attempt on her 26th birthday, and she abandoned her film career in 1973 to become an advocate for animal rights.

Ursula Andress

b.1936

Introduced to Hollywood as the 'new Dietrich' Ursula Andress never quite lived up to the comparison after her appearance as the first ever Bond Girl, opposite Sean Connery in *Dr. No* (1962). The image of the ultimate '60s blonde bombshell rising up out of the sea as the bikini-clad Honey Rider was perhaps her finest cinema moment.

A few films, and numerous affairs with male co-stars later, Andress went the *Playboy* route, boosting her career by posing for a nude centrefold in the magazine. This put paid to any possibility of her film career being taken seriously, affording her status as one of the most memorable poster girls instead.

Jane Birkin

b.1946

'Je t'aime,' breathed British actress Jane Birkin in the '60s hit of the same name, making her audiences squirm with delight (or embarrassment). The song, which became a hit for Birkin and her musician husband Serge Gainsbourg (or Serge Forward as he was jokingly referred to at the time), was banned on BBC radio due to its overtly sexual tones. Like it or not, the song left behind a legacy, which today is enjoying a renaissance in remixes the world over.

In addition to her breathy vocal abilities Birkin exhibited a gamine-like quality, which first made an appearance in Michelangelo Antonioni's cult film *Blow Up* (1966). The film was the first commercial release to represent the orgy of youth culture of '60s Britain in all its hedonistic glory. Subsequently, it too was censored. Birkin went on to appear in films throughout the '70s and '80s, including an adaptation of Agatha Christie's *Evil Under the Sun* (1981) starring Peter Ustinov.

Juliette Binoche

b.1964

Perhaps best known for her Oscar-winning role in *The English Patient* (1996), Juliette Binoche's natural beauty and seductive aura, combine with a sad, lovelorn character to contribute to her status as the most fêted of all contemporary French actresses. Her chosen roles, which she calls her 'sorrowful sisters', regularly focus on damaged, closed-off characters that are cool and enigmatic with a hint of vulnerability, and her reputation has mainly been based on intense, unglamorous roles in art house films. She is yet to star in a Hollywood production but says of the decision 'I want to tell a story I believe in.'

Before turning to films at the age of 20, Binoche was a regular on the stage, performing with the Conservatoire de Paris. Her vulnerability, combined with her open, vibrant nature has seen her flit from film to fashion, replacing Isabella Rossellini as the face of Lancôme in the company's advertising campaign for the perfume Poême. According to the cosmetics giant, she was chosen for her 'astonishing ability to express two things at once: tranquillity on the surface, fire and passion inside.'

Marilyn Monroe

1926-1962

Not much can be written about Marilyn Monroe that hasn't already been said. Her breathless sexuality, blonde bombshell looks and voluptuous figure earned her star status, but it was her humorous intelligence, her struggle for recognition as more than just another pretty face and finally, her tragic death which made her a Hollywood legend.

Monroe's enduring image is the famous scene in the film *The Seven Year Itch* (1954), where her white halter-necked dress is blown up in a gust of air from a subway grating. Over 2,000 spectators, and several hundred photographers gathered in New York to watch and record her as she posed for the scene for over two hours.

Much of her appeal lies in her vulnerability, and though it was noted that she was a talented comedienne, with a superb sense of timing, she never had an ego problem. 'I knew how third-rate I was,' she said of her acting ability. 'I could actually feel my lack of talent, as if it were cheap clothes I was wearing inside.' One reporter commented, 'There is about her a waif-like quality, an underlying note of pathos which can be strangely moving.'

Isabella Rossellini

b.1952

Still stunning at 40, Lancôme nevertheless decided to replace her as the face of its cosmetics empire with a younger model. Not to be outdone, she subsequently developed her own cosmetics line.

The daughter of famed Italian film director Roberto Rossellini and legendary Swedish actress Ingrid Bergman, Isabella Rossellini seemed perfectly suited to the screen, with dark, sultry and mysterious looks most women would kill for.

Initially, however, Rossellini didn't plan on pursuing her family's example, and it wasn't until she had worked as both model and television reporter that she finally succumbed to her natural calling, with an appearance in *White Nights* (1985). *Blue Velvet* (1986), directed by David Lynch followed. 'David Lynch came out of it a genius, and I came out of it a fat girl. I'm sorry that the only comment I get about the part is the way I look,' was what she had to say on the subject.

Rossellini reportedly enjoys disparaging her perfect looks and poise, choosing roles in quirky films and appearances on TV's *Friends* and *Merlin*.

Christy Turlington

b.1969

One of the much-hyped Supermodels of the
glamorous '80s, Christy Turlington's exotic looks,
which she inherited from her Salvadoran mother,
are still hailed as timeless across the world today.

Turlington began her career at the age of 14
when a photographer spotted her horse-riding
near her home in Miami. Ten years later, she was
immortalised in plastic, as the 'prototype' for 120
mannequins commissioned by the Metropolitan
Museum of Modern Art in New York. Calvin Klein
also recognised her qualities. In 1989, Turlington
signed an exclusive contract for *Eternity* perfume.

Lauren Bacall

b.1924

After her
Hollywood
debut, James
Agee wrote
of Bacall
'She has
a javelin-like
vitality, a
fierce female
shrewdness,
and a special
sweet
sourness...
plus a
clothes-counting
self-confidence...
and a
trombone
voice'

Lauren Bacall's aura is one of glamour heightened with a worldly confidence which, as a young actress in her twenties, she projected far beyond her years. The perfect combination of sultriness and common sense, Bacall first made waves in the world of modelling when, at the age of 19, she appeared on the cover of *Harpers Bazaar*.
The result drew the attention of Hollywood and it wasn't long before 'The Look', as she became known, was gracing the silver screen.

Her debut film saw her cast opposite one of the biggest male stars of the day, and her subsequent marriage to Humphrey Bogart sealed her fame, not only for her magnetic presence on screen, but also as the woman who turned a fantasy love affair into reality. Women everywhere tried to emulate Bacall's self-assured, seductive image.

After marrying her beloved 'Bogie', Bacall put her career on hold, only returning to acting, on stage this time, after his death. William Faulkner summed up her lasting appeal perfectly, with the toast: 'To Lauren Bacall, who was not satisfied with just being a pretty face, but who rather decided to prevail.'

Ingrid Bergman

1915-1982

When Bergman left her husband for Rossellini, she was even denounced on the floor of the US Senate, who saw her as 'Hollywood's apostle of degradation'.

'Of all the gin joints in all the towns in all the world, she walks into mine.' So said Humphrey Bogart of Ingrid Bergman, and the whole world swooned in agreement. One of the hottest female stars of '40s Hollywood, Bergman's intriguing accent, luminous beauty and superb acting talent ensured that every film she touched after *Casablanca* (1943) turned to gold.

Her personal life, tainted with tragedy, gave her a certain sexy vulnerablity, which made her all the more appealing. Until she was touched by scandal, that is. In the '50s, Bergman left her husband and daughter for Italian film director Roberto Rossellini and even though they married and had twins, Isabella and Isotta, her pure and wholesome image was shattered. In typical Bergman style, however, she survived the affair with dignity, and the outrage didn't last long. Later years saw her popularity increase again. 'People didn't expect me to have emotions like other women', she said.

Catherine Deneuve

b.1943

Archetypal icy blonde, Catherine Deneuve's French chic and pristine elegance is as apparent in French fashion and perfume houses as it is in her films.

The face of Chanel during the '80s, Deneuve began her acting career at the tender age of 13. By 16 she was the protégée of filmmaker Roger Vadim (ex-husband and 'creator' of Brigitte Bardot). But it was *Repulsion* (1965), Roman Polanski's first English film, in which she played a sexually repressed schizophrenic, that saw her first achieve international acclaim. Polanski described her as a 'professional virgin, but sexy'.

Her steely feminine persona led to her being typecast in later films as the strong independent type, and this was literally cast in stone in 1985, when her profile was chosen as the model for the symbol of the French Republic.

Designer Yves Saint-Laurent, who upholds the actress as his one-time muse says of her 'She is a woman who makes me dream.'

Patti Smith

b.1946

Punk priestess Patti Smith is one of rock's most influential musicians. Her celebration of feminine desire and defiance inspired her fans to find a new way of expressing, rather than just dressing themselves. Her influence on the world of fashion can be attributed in part to photographer Robert Mapplethorpe.

Currently enjoying resurgence in cosmopolitan youth culture, the punk look embodied by Smith in the '70s was strikingly captured by Mapplethorpe for her first Patti Smith Group album covers. The pair shared a room in New York's notorious Chelsea Hotel for some time, and Smith's debut recording, 'HeyJoe/Piss Factory', was partly financed by the photographer.

Michael Stipe of REM commented 'Her influence today is undeniable. There's not anybody I know in a band anywhere who does not revere the records that she put out. There was a rawness and energy to *Horses* that I had not heard in any other music.'

Picture Credits

Every possible effort has been made to attribute all photographic credits as accurately as possible. In the instance of any mistakes or omissions, Absolute Press would like to offer their apologies and ask that misrepresented parties bring any such errors to our attention.